MAKING
STORIES

IRENE N. WATTS

MAKING STORIES

HEINEMANN
Portsmouth, NH

© 1992 Pembroke Publishers Limited
528 Hood Road
Markham, Ontario
L3R 3K9

Published in the U.S.A. by
Heinemann Educational Books, Inc.
361 Hanover Street
Portsmouth, NH 03801-3959
ISBN (U.S.) 0-435-08614-6

Canadian Cataloguing in Publication Data

Watts, Irene N.,
  Making stories

Includes bibliographical references and index.
ISBN 0-921217-73-0

1. English language – Composition and exercises –
Study and teaching (Elementary). I. Title.

LB1576.W37 1992   372.6'23   C92-093088-3

Editor: Art Hughes
Design: John Zehethofer
Cover Photography: Ajay Photographics
Typesetting: Jay Tee Graphics Ltd.

Printed and bound in Canada
9 8 7 6 5 4 3 2 1

For Meghan, Rebeccah, Sarah,
Jean-Michel, and Matthew

Acknowledgments

Bob Barton and David Booth for the quotation from *Stories in the Classroom* (Pembroke Publishers Limited, 1990).

Dionne Brand for permission to reprint ''The Bottleman'' from *Earth Magic* (Kids Can Press, 1979).

Contents

Introduction

I am sitting with a group of children talking about the first stories they remember. Their ages range from 9-16. Mark, 9, says, "I don't remember being told *any* bedtime stories. When I started to read, about four years ago, I liked bears." Carmen, 16, remembers an endless story her father told her every night at bedtime, about a little girl who goes skipping off into the woods and meets all her favorite animals — the frog, the deer, and the hoot owl. Each asks her the same question, "Why aren't you asleep?" She recites the ritual word for word.

Most children are read to at home, in school, in libraries, any place where children congregate, long before they learn to read for themselves. Later, children read widely for their own pleasure. The young child makes up imaginative adventures and long rambling tales, but somehow this facility gets lost early in life, or it is not actively fostered. Making up new stories happens less frequently as children get older.

Storytelling is not as common as the reading of an existing story. Children listen to professional storytellers from time to time but, unfortunately, it is usually a special occasion, something out of the ordinary.

Children creating stories orally, the words spoken with the thought's immediacy for the very first time and shared by a few or by many, is the process described in *Making Stories*.

The creation of hitherto untold stories encourages language, imagination, spontaneity, confidence, a grasp of plot, and a sense of tension and drama. The storyteller explores the universe and creates new characters and myths, making sense of the world. In any size of grouping from two to 30, cultural experiences are exchanged and increasing status afforded those among us still struggling with spoken or written forms.

Children are very much aware of this growing confidence in words. Here is how Robin (age 12) puts it:

> One day I was on holiday with my family at Yellowstone Park. I was about five. One night we were sleeping, and I heard a scraping outside. I got up and looked around and saw a bear at a picnic table. I got scared, but I already knew he couldn't smell me because the wind was blowing into my face. The scent wasn't being carried towards him (I forgot how I learned this) and I was out of sight. I looked around and saw a man lying down, but still alive, because he coughed. The bear didn't hear. After a while the bear left. I looked at the man, but he just got up slowly and said "Whew!" and left. I went inside and flopped into bed. Later on I told the whole story, when I could get the right words. *I wasn't good with words then.*

"A storyteller is like a car which needs fuel." (Solomon Rushdie in *Haroun and the Sea of Stories*)

A few years ago Bevan (age 9) wrote to me as he struggled to put into words that he, or the assignment he had been given, lacked 'fuel'.

> I'm sitting here and I don't know what to do. It's a stupid composition. Read a story, answer questions. *What* questions? I *sat* here for five minutes. Finally, after she answered everybody's questions she asked *me* and I replied, "What questions do we answer?" Boy, was I mad.

What do we make up stories about? Where do we find the 'fuel'?

Journal or diary entries are a natural and ready source. So are holidays and festivals, birthdays and special events.

Fears, hopes, dreams.

Science fiction.

Newspapers and magazines.

Nightmares.

The environment.

Siblings and families.

Schools and friends.

The creative writing talents of children are a frequent source of wonder to teachers, even though there may be days when, like Bevan, there is neither inspiration nor inclination to write. Inspiration doesn't always come instantly nor does it remain a constant 'fuel'. Writing is a very private and mostly individual occupation. For some children the mechanics of writing are difficult, or their language is not yet fluent enough to make the setting down of ideas and experiences a joyful task.

Creating stories orally is an additional tool for the variety of oral and written language experiences so prevalent in today's classrooms. It is also an enjoyable recreational activity that can take place anywhere and at any time.

Making up stories may be an individual, pair, group, or whole class activity. Any size group and any age can participate. Like journal writing, inspiration comes from many sources. Group story making is a jazz form where one note or musical passage inspires another musician to take up the theme and play a variation upon it. In story making there is a similar sharing of words, ideas, and responsibility for the story. The tale flows as thought, because at the time of creation the mechanics of writing are not involved.

Questions to motivate a beginning are as varied as the stories themselves. There is no right or wrong way to start or any preconceived way to end.

What does this (sound, object, picture) make you think of?

Who wore, carried, found, sold, bought, or lost this?

The story ends with the words "No More." Who wants to begin it?

"Someone was walking along the path. Suddenly. . . ." Now finish the story.

Who has an idea to start a story?

What happens now? Let's go round the circle so that everyone can add a bit to the story. Just say "pass" if you're not quite ready.

The discussion, the talking, the questions are different each time. The story will surprise, illuminate, disappoint, shock, touch, or convulse the listener with laughter, or perhaps not at all! The story may be created in 5 minutes or 15, or 50, or it may take many days. It may be retold, reworked, dramatized, mimed, chanted, painted, or written down. It may be the creation of one person, two friends working together, or 20 voices finding a common thread.

Making Stories shares some ways to begin the oral story making process.

1

"And the rabbit's name is Shadow."

The group is made up of 24 children ages five to seven. I had not met the class before. We sit on the floor, and I am part of the circle. I have brought a brown furry hand puppet, a rabbit, the same size as a real baby one. It has blue eyes, is soft and very lifelike. As I hold it we begin talking about pets. The conversation covers every single child's pet: past (including fish that died), present, and future hopes of ownership.

One child says, "I'm going to get a dog for my birthday." I share the fact that I live in an apartment and sadly am not permitted to keep a pet.

After perhaps ten minutes of such exchange, when the good talk has given us a bond, I begin something like this: "Let's make up a story about the rabbit. I'll pass it around the circle so you can all have a turn holding it and thinking up a name." In this way, before the story even gets started, everyone contributes. The children each offer a name as they handle the puppet: Brownie, Thumper, Cottontail, Peter, Fluffy, Shadow, Smoky.

I choose one of the names, recalling a few in the process and focusing on the puppet so that it almost seems the rabbit's own choice.

Next, I ask questions that will give me an indication as to the kind of story the children are ready to tell, or in this instance to share in the telling with me.

I might ask:

Where do you want Shadow to live?

Does he belong to someone, or does he live by himself?

Is he tame or wild?

What kind of adventures might he have?

Perhaps I ask:

Does he go on a journey?

What do you think scares him?

Four or five questions usually provide answers to start us off. I begin the story with "Shadow lived in. . ." and then pause for suggestions and choices that will make the story belong to the class. A sense of ownership is important here. In the following sample of this technique, commonly known as 'filling in the gaps', the italicized words are the children's actual suggestions.

Filling in the gaps

THE STORY OF SHADOW

Shadow lived in . . . *a wooden hutch in Meghan's yard.* Every day Meghan . . . *played with Shadow — before school, after school, and even when it rained.* She fed him . . . *water, carrots, and lettuce,* and at the end of every day she remembered to . . . *bolt the hutch door.*

One evening when she was letting Shadow run on the grass, Meghan's mother called her in for supper. It was her favorite, . . . *spaghetti.* Meghan quickly put Shadow in the hutch, and hurried inside to eat. She was really hungry. But she forgot . . . *to bolt the hutch door.*

In the middle of the night Meghan woke up, because . . . (At this point there are many different ideas — a big cat, a noise, thunder, a ghost, she fell out of bed, etc. I make a fast choice, trying to accept several suggestions.) . . . *she heard rain and thunder and a door banging,* and she remembered that . . . *she had forgotten to shut the hutch door.* Meghan got out of bed immediately and put on her . . . *water boots* and . . . *went downstairs into the yard.* The hutch door was swinging open and closed, back and forth. Meghan put her hand inside the hutch. It was . . . *empty!*

ME: What did she do?

She looked all over and called, "Shadow! Shadow!" But the wind was blowing hard, the trees looked as though they were moving, and the rain was coming down harder and harder. Suddenly there was a crack of thunder and . . . *a flash of lightning* and Meghan was very scared. She wanted . . . *to find Shadow*, but she also wanted . . . *to go back inside and tell her mother.*

ME: Where could Shadow be?

In the woods.

When Meghan ran inside to get her supper, Shadow didn't want to . . . *go to sleep.* He pushed . . . *his nose against the hutch door*, and when it opened . . . *he hopped out!* He liked . . . *the juicy grass, and the smells* and the . . . *worms.* When it got dark, he was far away from home. When the storm began, he . . . *got scared and ran all over the yard*, and under the gate and . . . *into the woods* across the street.

In the woods there were . . . *snakes, frogs, mice and wolverines, and bears and raccoons.* When the lightning flashed . . . *Shadow hid under a big tree*, trembling with fear.

Meghan was cold and wet, too, but she had to find Shadow. She went back into the house to get . . . *her raincoat and the flashlight on the refrigerator.*

She didn't . . . *wake up her mum.*

Meghan went outside again and decided to . . . *cross the street.* When she was in the woods, she called out . . . *"Shadow! Shadow!"* A big bolt of lightning lit up the whole woods, and just before it got dark again, Meghan saw . . . *Shadow hiding under the tree.* Meghan forgot to be scared. She turned on the flashlight and . . . *Shadow saw her and ran to her.* Then she . . . *picked him up and ran back home.*

The light was on in the kitchen, and Meghan's dad was there. He was so . . . (again many choices — glad, angry, happy, scared, etc.) . . . *glad to see her he yelled!* Then he . . . *dried them both with a big towel*, and . . . *Meghan's mum made hot chocolate.* Shadow went to sleep . . . *on Meghan's* bed, just for one night. Meghan never again forgot . . . *to bolt the hutch door.* She also promised she would never go out at night by herself again!

Comment

The gap technique demonstrated here is a simple yet effective way of creating stories with young children. All that one needs is a basic story framework and patience.

The rabbit puppet seems to inspire many adventures of independence and running away. A small furry mouse, a lion hand puppet, or a ceramic bird on a stick inspire similar intriguing adventures.

Other ways to begin

To make a small furry mouse, I attach a small piece of fur with a tail to a 30 cm (12″) piece of dowel.

ME: What does this look like?
CLASS: A mouse.
ME: Is it a brave mouse, or is it timid and shy?
CLASS: Shy.
ME: Does the mouse live in the city, in a barn in a farmyard, or out in a field?

There is always a variety of answers. Some children might not respond at all to the line of questioning, as the following response demonstrates.

STUDENT: My grandpa kept a mouse in a shoebox when he was little.
ME: Has anyone here ever kept a mouse?

How we start is not as important as accepting the children's responses and somehow incorporating as many of them as possible in *our* story.

I usually begin a story with the lion puppet by passing around the puppet, which is soft and lifelike, the size of a small puppy.

ME: What kind of noise does a lion make?

(The class makes roaring sounds — little encouragement required!)

ME   (Seriously) Suppose the lion didn't know how to roar. What kind of noise might it make?

The story will be different each time, depending on the responses. One student, for example, didn't wait for the second part of the question and after "how to roar" immediately responded, "Find someone to teach him."

In this case I began like this: "Every animal in the jungle looked at the baby lion and admired him. The tiger spoke first: 'He's *very* quiet!' Then the tiger made a tremendous roar." Children participate by making appropriate sounds, and the story proceeds with the task of finding a way to give the lion a voice. Eventually, in order to save a friend caught in a trap, it roars to summon help.

In another instance when I asked, after a while, "What kind of noise might the baby lion make?" this is the response I got:

STUDENT: A kitten.

ME: This is the story of Leo who sounded like a kitten and lived in a circus, etc.

For children over seven, the puppet is simply passed around the circle, and the story, after the initial talking and questions, is created entirely by the group. If the story seems to bog down, inserting a question, such as "What did Shadow do when the big rock blocked his escape?" usually helps the flow.

I find that repeating the children's responses gives them importance, even if their ideas can not be included in the final story.

ME: Have you ever seen someone ill-treat a pet?

STUDENT: I saw a boy throwing stones at ducks in a pond.

ME: Throwing stones!

Extensions

Sometimes I suggest that the children paint a cover illustration for the story. Then singly, in pairs, or in small groups they physically represent the picture. From this first still picture, I encourage groups to illustrate other key incidents or moments physically.

The storm, the search for Shadow, and other important happenings in the story may be dramatized by the class following the making of the story. This happens with the class working as individuals, but all at the same time, while the teacher narrates. Groups of children may select portions of the story to act out. Dramatizing the story is as natural a process as painting the story.

2

"Listen! I can hear . . ."

I collect sounds. Some sound making instruments that work particularly well for group story making are a small goat-skin drum from Peru, an African hippo drum, a Chinese wooden rattle (kokoriku); bells of different sizes and shapes, in particular a string of Indian bells; a small Mexican pottery bird that is really a whistle and sounds just like a loon; a clay ocarina, an American song whistle with a deep tone; different sized pebbles, a pair of cherrywood sticks, a kalimba. I use these in conjunction with different surfaces, and with everyday sounds, such as a sigh, a whisper, a cry for help, a door slamming, a chair overturning, a foot dragging, a hand clap.

We form our customary story circle, either sitting on the floor or on chairs. The group is any age from preschool to adult.

We may begin with a short listening game. Veda, a music student, moves around whistling softly. She sounds like a bird, and everyone points in the direction of the sound, keeping their eyes closed. We might (again with eyes closed) count the beats heard in an intricate drum pattern, or discuss what footsteps sound like as someone moves across the circle in different styles of movement.

We talk about sounds, starting with the first remembered ones:

- My mother laughing or singing downstairs.
- The mobile fluttering above my head.
- A train whistling in the distance.
- My sister practising piano scales — over and over again.

We talk about sounds heard on the way to school, or favorite sounds: cats purring, rain on the window pane, the quiet when you're tucked up in bed. Disliked sounds: tires squealing, balloons bursting, Dad yelling to get you up in the morning, taps dripping. Strange and mysterious sounds: footsteps along a lonely street, an owl hooting. Everyone has many contributions to make. Memory, imagination, and story ingredients are palpable in the room.

Responding to and interpreting sounds

I suggest some questions for the children to think about, reminding them to consider what quality of sounds they hear: angry, urgent, happy, sad. I ask them to think about who or what is responsible for the making of the sound, and who hears it. What is important about the sound?

I then make a sequence of three sounds, allowing time between each.

Example One	*Sounds used*
(Students keep their eyes closed.)	I scratch the surface of the goatskin drum with my nails.
	I overturn a chair violently.
	I whisper, ''Come in.''

It does not matter what the chosen sounds are, since any will be sufficient to draw responses from the group. Similarly, the questions to reflect on before listening are not part of a formula. The wording differs each time.
ME: Open your eyes. I would like to hear your ideas.
The students respond with:
- A bear is trying to get in.
- He's after food.
- Yes, there's a trapper in the cabin, and he runs to hide.
- No, to get his gun, and he knocks over a chair.

- I think it's the bear who knocks everything over.
- When the bear is nosing around, and the trapper is hiding, his friend knocks on the window and. . .

There is so much information that it's time to start the story.

ME: Who wants to start the story?

I hand the small drum I used for one of the sounds to a student to begin. The convention in this kind of story circle is established. The drum is handed around and sounded when the student has finished a portion of the story. This often establishes a sound rhythm. Sometimes it serves to highlight parts of the story. The students are told that if they have nothing to add at the time the drum is passed around, they may just say "pass" and sound the drum before passing it on. In this way everyone is still involved. Often the second time around a verbal contribution will be forthcoming.

If there is a strong disagreement about what the original sounds seem to be, we talk until we reach some consensus for a story basis.

Following is a story from an older group, ages 11-14, with some previous experience in story building:

Example Two	*Sounds used*
(Students keep their eyes closed.)	Fingers tapping on the table. Five Indian bells on a string. Bird whistle.

The responses are fairly similar, ranging from temple bells to ghosts to spirits to warnings. The setting is a jungle or a haunted house.

The 17 students, one complete story circle, respond:

- The temple bell in the jungle village was ringing and ringing.
- Everyone ran towards the temple.
- Bad news again.
- The people in the village had been afraid for a long time.

- Every week people went into the jungle and didn't come back.
- No one knew why. Maybe this time there would be an answer.
- Pass. [Bells are sounded by the 'passing' student.]
- But far away.
- Inside the jungle, deep, deep, deep.
- There is a haunted place.
- At the meeting it was decided that the children were forbidden to leave their homes and yards. The temple has spoken.
- Two friends who were not afraid decided to find out the secret of the haunted place.
- That night Abe tapped on the window of his friend Nandi.
- They went quietly around the houses and soon there were five more kids ready to go.
- It was dark. There was no moon.
- It was quiet.
- A bird rustled in the trees. They almost screamed and gave themselves away.
- Suddenly they heard an eerie whistling sound. It sounded human and came from every corner of a tumbledown hut.

The story continues with the group entering the haunted place, where walls are tumbling down and covered with creepers that look like snakes.

- Maybe they are snakes (contribution from the student who had passed on the previous round).
- The whistling is caused by a ghost which inhabits the place and lures people deeper and deeper into the jungle.
- The children are rescued by their elders, and the remains of the house are burned to the ground.

The story ends with one student saying:

- The bells of the temple rang to celebrate the safe return of the children.

Example Three	Sounds used
(Students close their eyes.)	Hands rubbed together. The slam of a door. Silence.

I ask the students to find a place by themselves so that they can concentrate on the sound I'm going to make. I explain that I want them to use their imagination to suggest ideas about the sound. I make the first sound and allow a few moments for the students to respond. I ask them to move to another person (if numbers are unequal they may work in threes). Together they share their thoughts about the first sound. I ask them to listen, again with eyes closed, to a second sound, and a third one. Again a little time is allowed before they discuss their responses together.

At this point the pair moves to another couple and they share all their responses to date. I ask them to build a short story around those ideas. Because there are now four or possibly five people involved, they will have to agree on using the ideas that will work best in their group story. They may choose one new sound to add drama to the story, if they need it.

I remind them to decide where and when the story happens, who or what is important, and what or whose story they are telling.

The story may be told by one person at a time or by the entire group in chorus. However, everyone must contribute in some way, using words and/or sound effects and choosing a title for their story.

The following story was created by Paula, Nathalie, Rachel, and Miranda, ages 13-15.

THE SINGING GHOST

Two sisters live in a big heritage house with an attic over the wing where they sleep. Every night they can hear singing coming from the loft. It is an eerie sound, and it only happens when the girls are alone in their room. They tell their parents, who naturally don't believe them.

"You're just imagining it. You've been watching too many horror movies on TV." But it is not their imagination, and they can't sleep because of the sound.

After many instances of the parents coming into their room to listen and hearing nothing, the girls become so terrified that the parents decide to open the attic door, which has been sealed shut for many years. When they go up the narrow steps and enter the attic, they find an old brass bed, two chairs, and a chest of drawers with a mirror. The furniture is all very old and dusty.

When they look in the mirror they see a young lady brushing her long hair and hear her singing an eerie lullaby. This was the singing that had frightened the girls.

The next day the family leaves the house. No one lives there any more, except. . . .

The story is then dramatized by the group.

Example Four   *Sound used*
(Children close their   An African kalimba
eyes.)

The students respond:
• Water.
• Deer.
• Magic.
• River.

When I have three or four responses that the children seem to like, I begin the story, with the understanding that they are to help me whenever I sound the kalimba.

I encourage their input throughout to help them develop a sense of ownership. The four or five basic thoughts inspired by the original sounds must be included, because these are what the children have felt the story should be about. Here are the opening paragraphs with the children's actual words italicized:

This is a story about a river. It starts high in the mountains, where rivers begin. The water in the river is [kalimba sounds] *magic*. Yes, whoever drinks from the river will be granted [kalimba] *one wish*. The river flows down the mountain and ends in a pool which is full of magic water. Who knows about the magic in the water? [kalimba] *Frogs, birds, fish, deer.* They all know about the magic, but no one else does, and if they talked about it, it doesn't matter because no one can understand them.

One day someone was walking through the woods [kalimba]: *A little girl.* She was feeling [kalimba] *sad* because [kalimba] (several responses) *she was lonely, too small, poor, wanted her pet to get well.*

(At this point there are more ideas to choose from than we need, so I decide on one that seems appropriate at the time — *lonely*.)

The lonely little girl sees a small deer trying to drink water from the pool, but there are only a few drops left. She coaxes the deer to come to her. [kalimba]

This is the moment to pair up the children and let them finish the story. Threes work well too. When each story has been privately decided on, the storytellers are given the kalimba to hold and sound while they finish the story. This strategy takes at least two sessions.

Extensions for sound stories
Children may make up their own stories, choosing their own sound effects, but limiting the sounds to one or two — or having unlimited choice. Listeners are required to identify the sounds.

One group creates sounds for *another* group to interpret in a story.

Groups are given an envelope which contains a card on which there is listed a character, a sound, and an opening or closing line. They then complete the story. Following is an example:

Character: an old shepherd.
Sound: a wolf howl.
Opening: The snow is deep. Don't go out tonight, please.
Closing: Nothing can get through the drifts.

These activities often result in 'radio plays' in which the actors are listened to but not seen.

Comment
The use of different sounds as a basis for new stories and drama is one of my own preferred ways of beginning. Sound works particularly well with mixed age groups and in classrooms where English is a second language. The making of sounds and response to them are basic and universal and help story participants by making them focus on an external, non-threatening device.

3

What's their story?

As a storyteller of an existing story, I like to hold up something that will symbolize the theme, both for the audience and for myself. It may be a gold mask for a story of a family who worship the sun; a carving of a small bird for the Japanese story "The Tale of the Tongue-cut Sparrow;" a piece of smooth soapstone in the shape of a seal for "The Selkie." A simple cap suffices for the many stories of magic hats which enable the wearer to understand the language of birds and animals.

The objects may represent animals or humans, gods or spirits; they may stand for an idea, a civilization, a philosophy, a culture, or a force of nature.

Using objects for inspiration

My searches for just the right object to fit someone else's story is quite a different process from looking for objects to encourage story building, where it is the mask, or bird, or brass mirror that inspires the process of creating a new story. Everything has potential for a new story. Objects I like to use include: a crystal paperweight, an antique sand pail, a red balloon, a miniature gold brass rocking chair (doll's house size), a brass cat, a speckled feather, a string of beads, an old coin, a Balinese frog mask.

I find my treasures in flea markets and garage sales, antique stores, and art galleries. I comb the beach for pieces of driftwood that might suggest animal or human features. An airline ticket with an exotic destination, a foreign matchbox, pieces of unusual fabric, candles and candlesticks — all of these become valuable tools for the story maker.

Erika (Grade 1) is inspired to begin a story. Because we are sitting on the floor on small new squares of colored carpet, she says: "Suddenly the carpet moved. All the children jumped as the carpet floated up and flew out through the window. . . ."

At a garage sale at our local community theatre, I found an oversized papier-mâché gold key which had been made for a Christmas pantomime. It was only $2.00 worth of gold paint and paper, but it has yielded years of stories. I pass the key around the circle and ask, "What does this key unlock?"

The responses are immediate — some predictable but some unusual:

• A safe.
• Dreams.
• A castle dungeon.
• An adventure.
• A treasure cave.
• A nightmare.
• A secret.
• A cupboard door.

"Who owns it/lost it/stole it/needs it?" The replies give us the story beginnings. Later we may investigate other people's stories about keys: *The Secret Garden* or *Alice in Wonderland*.

Sometimes I put an old canvas sack full of different objects on the floor in the middle of the story circle. We have already decided what kind of story technique we are going to use — a one-word-each story. On other occasions, students may prefer a one-sentence-each telling. All ages enjoy both methods.

I close my eyes slowly in a familiar ritual and point to

a child. The child indicated puts a hand into the sack and draws out an object: a silver slipper, an old map, a carved stick, a clown nose. The child looks at the object for perhaps 15 seconds, and begins.

The following is the start of a one-word story:

Once
an
old
clown
left
the
circus.
He
had
nowhere
to
go.
He
had
nothing
left
except
his
red
clown
nose.
He
went
to
a
town
and
sat
on
the
curb.
He

put
on
the
nose.
A
dog
licked
his
hand.

I sometimes pair interesting objects with related or contrasting qualities. For a group of 26 students there will be at least 14 sets of objects. I put them on the floor or on a large table, displaying them on a bright piece of cloth. To set a mood I may darken the room and illuminate the objects with just one light.

Groupings are as varied as possible to inspire all kinds of storytelling. I may pair:

— a baseball bat and a $1.00 bill
— a painted wooden duck and a large, green glass marble
— an owl carved out of the root of a tree with a frog
— a latch key and a pair of dark glasses
— a small ceramic dragon (Christmas tree ornament) and a miniature, paper flower bouquet
— a bus ticket and a torn wallet
— a Japanese fan and small Asian mask
— a small bright fish on a stick and a piece of fish net
— a piece of oily rope and a bird feather
— a snake and a ring
— a small battered suitcase and a muffler
— a miniature pair of figures in a glass container with a wooden log cabin or stove
— a thimble and a white glove
— an antique photo and a lace handkerchief
— a magnifying glass and a small leather-bound dictionary or book

Students walk around in pairs or threes and are given

time to examine the paired objects. They are then asked to select the items which they want to make a story about. Alternatively, I may discourage talk at this stage and let the children investigate individually before asking them to move to the objects which interest them. Stories may be told alone, in twos, or in threes. Experienced groups have been asked to consider objects which do not appeal to them immediately. Sometimes this approach creates quite unusual stories.

I remind them that their objects can be any size they want, of lifelike or vast as well as tiny proportions. I ask them to consider the best way of sharing the telling of the story, to think of a title, and to have a strong opening and closing sentence.

I remind them that we need to know why the story has to be told, whose story it is, and the importance of the objects they have chosen. What is it that brings them together: dislike, friendship, forces outside their control? What is the problem or conflict that needs to be resolved in the story?

Example One
Objects: A piece of real fish net and a miniature yellow fish
          placed on a blue cloth of shimmering material.
Storytellers: Matthew (9), Mary Jane (11), Amanda (13).
Mary Jane narrates the story. Amanda and Matthew act it out during the telling and make storm sounds.

OCEAN FRIENDS
This story is about the ocean and a golden fish who are friends. They have been friends for a long time and use the waves to play hide-and-go-seek. They play all day long, in rough and calm water. One day a boat came and cast its net into the sea. The fish was careless and got caught. The boat sailed away. The ocean's friend was gone forever. They would never play together again. The next day when the boat returned without the fish, the ocean made a great storm and sank the boat.

Example Two

Objects: A painted wooden duck and a glass marble.

Storytellers: Ashley (9), and Heather (8½).

ASHLEY: A duck lived on a pond in the middle of the woods.

HEATHER: It was safe there, and she had lots to eat.

ASHLEY: One day machines came and there was a lot of noise. All the animals and birds left except the duck. She hid and laid some eggs and stayed there.

HEATHER: Soon all the trees were gone.

ASHLEY: Workers built a mall with glass walls. When the ducks came out of the eggs, there was nothing to eat and nowhere to swim.

HEATHER: One night there was a storm which broke the glass walls.

ASHLEY: Workers came to clean up. They found the family of ducks and put them in their truck.

HEATHER: The ducks were scared, but the truck stopped at a nice park.

ASHLEY: The workers put the ducks in a pond where they were safe and had clean water and food.

Extension

Students enjoy becoming an object, speaking with the object's voice and telling its story. The doll's house chair is a starting point for all kinds of chair stories: rocking chair, cinema seat, park bench, high chair, dentist chair, deck chair, desk chair, porch chair. Students in pairs or singly speak with the voice of a chair that has observed and seated the world for many years, or is new to the job. Poignant and hilarious dialogue frequently results, mostly quite spontaneous (after the kind of chair and where it is to be found have been decided by the students).

In pairs, students tell their tales as garbage cans, playground equipment, old dolls, and favorite sneakers.

4

Secrets

With a class of 10-to-12-year-olds, I sit in our customary story circle, in the centre of which lies a shell on a dark green silky remnant of material. We begin by passing the shell around. Each person listens to the shell for a short while. Then I ask, "What do you hear?"

The students respond with:
- The wind.
- The ocean.
- The waves.
- Seagulls.
- A storm.
- A rushing sound.

Revealing imaginary secrets

I replace the shell and say, "The shell has been lying at the bottom of the sea for hundreds of years. It has heard many secrets whispered by the wind and the water, by fish and by fishermen and deep-sea divers. Think about the kind of secrets you would hear and keep if you were the shell."

I allow sufficient time for the process to work.

"Now think about just one secret, and when you are ready, draw or write about it on the mural paper." A large sheet of paper, big enough for everyone to work on, and a supply of drawing and writing materials are ready. The group works simultaneously. I may play Debussy's *Les Nocturnes–la Mer* in the background.

Together we talk about the secrets of the shell:
- seaweed that destroys pollution
- a fish that swallowed a magic wishing ring that still has one wish left
- a piece of glass that tells the future and that is buried under a rock
- a picture of a space alien's helmet
- a rock that is solid gold
- a hidden city
- the location to a pirate's treasure
- a map to an undiscovered island
- a ruby necklace
- the time of the tides
- where the fog goes

Each description becomes a small story, and the mural inspires further stories, individual, group and class, both oral and written narratives. The drawing, the writing, and the thinking time takes at least 20 minutes.

The following is a class story, the title of which was decided at the end of the telling.

THE WISHING RING

A boy was walking along the beach the morning after a great storm and there was a lot of wreckage lying around. He noticed something gleaming at the bottom of a rock pool. It was a fish, almost dead, barely moving. The boy scooped it up in his hands and saw that it had something caught in its throat. He shook it gently, shook it again, and something fell out onto the sand. The boy threw the fish back into the sea. It disappeared quickly.

Then he searched through the sand to find what had been stuck in the fish's throat. By the water's edge he saw a small ring. He quickly washed off the sand. It had a red jewel in it. "I can give this to my mum on her birthday next week." He ran home.

He could hardly wait to give it to her. On the morning of her birthday, he put it by her plate at breakfast time. She tried it on. It fitted perfectly. She said, "I've always wanted a ring like this, but I wish I had a necklace to go with it."

Suddenly around her throat a ruby necklace appeared. It must be a wishing ring! She tried wishing for more things — a house, a car, a bag of gold, but nothing happened. "It must have been the last wish left in the ring," she said. "It's the best present I ever had."

Sharing personal experiences

From there we go on to talking about different kinds of secrets, and create mystery stories and adventures. From fantasy and imagination, we move on to real life stories. Secrets are often very close to confessions because we share stories that we have never told anyone else before.

I ask students to bring in an oral tale that is a personal story, or one they have heard from someone close to them, a family member or friend.

Krista (age 12) tells about her first day at Kindergarten:

On my first day at Kindergarten, we had a resting time and I didn't know whether we had to sleep or just rest. So I thought I might as well sleep, so I lay down on my resting towel and started to sing to myself. I noticed everyone else was closing their eyes. So I closed my eyes too, and soon I fell asleep and dreamed that I was sleeping and everyone was watching me. Then I woke up and everyone in my class was sitting around me, making up a new version of Sleeping Beauty! I felt so stupid.

Mary Jane (age 11) tells about feeling envious:

A long time ago when I was about five, I was in a ballet of Cinderella. I was one of the horses. The instructor had put my class into two groups. Some were horses and the rest were elves. I was proud just to be in something. But the costumes for the elves were so beautiful! Although I had a bigger part than the elves, I still wished I could have been one.

Mia (age 13) tells about an experience of racism:

I always remember the first time I went to school in new blue jeans and a navy colored sweater. The teacher looked down and told the class my name. I looked up from staring at the floor and saw them all looking at me. Some of them were smiling at me. The teacher told me to sit down at a desk near the front. I could feel all the eyes behind me staring at my back. At recess I got in trouble with a gang and everybody in that gang started to tease me and spit at me. I ran away and went to my classroom. I cried and cried inside my deserted classroom and wiped away the tears when the bell rang.

After school I ran all the way home and cried for my mom. My mom hugged me and I told her about my day at school. She told me to feel brave and proud and if they bug me or tease me about being Oriental that I should tell the teacher.

The next day at school the gang bugged me again and I did what my mom said to do, and they got in so much trouble! They had to write lines and have a detention. As for me I made some nice friends. This happened to me when I was in Grade 4.

Wendy (age 11) tells about the scars on her right foot:

When I was a little kid at least two years old and my mom was giving me a bath, my mom went to get a towel from the hall cupboard. I reached over to get some dental floss that was on the counter so I could play with it. I was wrapping it around my toes. Then my mom came back and was trying to get the dental floss off of my toes but she couldn't and I was screaming so she got the nail scissors and tried to cut it off. She finally got it off but I had a huge cut in my toe and I still have a scar around my big and middle toes on my right foot.

Extensions

All the above examples are later dramatized, the student author working as director and filling in details.

Students sit in groups of their own choosing so that they will feel sufficiently comfortable to reveal their secret wishes. Each group then selects a wish, perhaps one that is common to the group, and creates a story of how the wish comes true or remains unfulfilled.

Retelling myths and folktales

We discuss the temptation to uncover secrets and the misfortunes that can result. Our reference may be to the Greek myth of Pandora, who was obsessed with curiosity about the sealed gold casket in her husband's home, which, when opened, unloosed every imaginable misfortune upon the world: disease, envy, sorrow beyond bearing; or of Prometheus stealing fire from the god Zeus to give to mankind, replacing man's warm skins and animal skill, and Zeus's terrible anger and punishment for the theft.

Students may wish to add stories from their own experiences after retelling the classic ones.

For a group of 11-to-14-year-olds I adapt the story "The Woman Who Would Be Wise." This is based on the legend of the seal, retold by Rowena Farre in *Seal Morning* (Hutchinson, Arrow Books, London).

THE WOMAN WHO WOULD BE WISE

A woman who lived by the sea longed above all else to understand the ocean's voice, for this would make her wise among her people. One night she invited a female seal to live with her. She promised to treat her as a daughter, and in return the seal would tell the woman the secrets of the ocean. The seal agreed to this arrangement.

Very soon thereafter the woman's advice was sought far and wide by fisherfolk who needed knowledge of tides, and storms, and shoals of fish, and the woman was well content.

* * *

One day the seal meets a young male seal, and they decide it is time for them to spend their lives together in the ocean, their true home. But when they tell the woman of their decision, even though the seal 'daughter' promises to return every month to give her 'land mother' the ocean's secrets, the woman persuades her to stay under her roof one more night.

That night marks the end of the seal's freedom, for while she sleeps, the woman ties a strongly woven rope around her neck, making her captive and allowing her only brief swims before dragging her back to land with her news of the ocean. One night in her struggles to free herself from the rope, the seal strangles and dies.

The woman, bitterly remorseful, spends the rest of her life alone (her fame evaporates overnight) in fear and guilt. The male seal, before he disappears beneath the waves, speaks the ocean's words to the woman: "Her spirit will come to me when I lie dying."

The woman dreads each passing day, fearing revenge from the ghosts of the seals. At last when the woman is near death she is allowed to see the seals (who have no thought but for each other) once more, and for one moment to understand the voice of the ocean which tells her she will be alone in death, as she was in life.

In the ensuing discussion, the students feel that the village people would never go near the cottage again for fear of ghosts. The seal's death (the seal is known to be a link between land and sea) is the breaking of a taboo. They decide to comment on the story as members of the community, taking different roles, some as elders who remember the episode, others as villagers who have heard only rumors of the event. They respond as follows:

- My mother always told me not to play on the beach near that house.
- She's right. A terrible crime happened there.
- My grandfather used to eat bannock and drink tea with the wise woman, while the seal would sleep on the rug like a cat.
- Yes, it was her pet. I'd see them walking on the sand every morning.
- Sometimes the seal had a fish in her mouth.
- On stormy nights the shadows of the dead seals ride on the top of the waves.
- They sit together on a rock in the moonlight.
- Her punishment was that the seals never again came to visit her.
- Our people knew of the storms and tides, but no more.
- She was very selfish, and her life became lonely and sad after the death of the seal.

The power of the story results in a different kind of retelling, a dramatic interpretation of how such a secret might impress the community for years to come. Retellings do not necessarily need to follow a plot line; they may be equally valuable for the insight the students experience and express, in other words, the effect of the story upon them and their understanding of life.

Exploring story through drama

A Grade 7 class was interested in the idea of the wise woman's fame disappearing "overnight" and wanted to explore what happened to the village people after the seal died.

We dramatized a scene in the woman's home (students volunteered to play seal and wise woman) with villagers crowded round, each bringing a small gift (mimed) as payment for information. They asked questions about the tides, mists, shoals of fish, and relatives lost at sea. The seal whispered the answers to the woman, who repeated them to the villagers.

I spoke as a narrator: "Time passed and the seal died."

Now we enacted the scene, after the death of the seal, where the woman groped for answers. After asking their questions, which were avoided or ignored, the students, as villagers, left, troubled.

The class formed groups and worked on events that happened to their families as a result of losing the seal's knowledge. Each group dramatized its story.

A Grade 5/6 class decided that the seal had left a legacy to the village. The students, in groups as people empowered with a special knowledge of the sea, dramatized how they were able to use this gift. One group narrated and acted out an encounter with a man-eating rogue shark that, as a result of the families' intervention, reverted to his true form of a prince. He had been transformed until such time as someone would look beyond fear and see the real person inside the shark.

5

Getting started

Students are asked to walk around the space and to think of an object. On a pre-arranged signal they freeze. I call a name at random and the student names the object.
HARRY: Window.

Students walk around the space again, this time directed to think of a character, either animal or human. They freeze. Once more I call a name at random and the student names the character.
KARIM: Dog.

Students walk again, this time directed to express in one word a problem or situation that may occur in a story.
STEPHANIE: Invisible.

Beginning with an object, a character, and a problem

Students group in threes to create a story using the three words proposed — *window, dog,* and *invisible.* They are given only a minute or two to talk about the basic outline before sharing the story with the rest of the class. Then the procedure begins again. This is a popular exercise in spontaneity and in working with fellow storytellers chosen at random.

Adding an emotion

Sometimes I ask for a *place*, a *character*, a *problem*, and an *emotion*. The procedure is similar to the one outlined above. The story almost tells itself.

The following outline comes from a group of 13-to-14-year-olds:

SARAH: Sidewalk.

BRIAN: Bag lady.

CARLA: Crime.

LES: Lonely.

Exchanging the telling

A more difficult extension is for each storyteller in the group to take turns in telling the opening, the events leading to the climax, the climax itself, and the conclusion. Each of the four participants is responsible for a different telling each time, until everyone has worked through the complete story. Of course the story changes with each telling.

Here are four different opening sentences for the *same* story:

SARAH: It was snowing.
The bag lady huddled under the cardboard pieces of her home under the viaduct.

BRIAN: The flashlight beamed onto the pile of rags that disguised the figure lying on the sidewalk. "Move along there!
Go on!"

CARLA: "Stop him! That's my purse. Stop, thief!"
But no one listened to the ramblings of the lonely figure pushing a shopping cart, piled high with plastic bags, along the sidewalk.

LES: Christmas Eve. "Here, buy yourself a dinner." The man put a twenty-dollar bill into the woman's hand and moved off, not waiting for her muttered thanks.

When the group has had time to tell its story in four different ways, the members decide which telling they would like to share with the rest of the class.

Creating alphabet lists

We create alphabet lists of words that immediately give ideas for stories. For example, I ask for three words beginning with the letter *a: ants, attic, apples.* We continue, the lists changing each time, depending on the age and interests of the class.

beautiful	balloon	bicycle
cat	cloud	climb
dinosaur	den	dream
emperor	egg	eye
fear	fall	fox
giant	ghost	gold
happy	hungry	human
iron	island	innocent
jelly	jewel	juniper
king	key	kill
lie	lost	lake
monster	marsh	magic
nightmare	never	nine
owl	open	orange
princess	pig	proud
quiet	queen	quest
rose	rich	run
street	steal	star
twins	terror	time
umbrella	ugly	uncle
veil	visitor	voice
water	wheel	wish
Xmas	X-ray	xylophone
year	yellow	yard
zoo	zone	zap

We use the lists in different ways. For example, a group of three can choose one word from the list that begins with the first letter of their names. Thus Mark, Karen and Leila may choose *monster, key,* and *lake* as three words to start them off on building a story. A student working alone might decide on the letter *p* and build the story using *pig, princess,* and *proud.* The lists provide an endless variety of possibilities for story building.

Composing starting sentences

I ask students to offer a sentence and to decide whether they would like it to be the beginning, the middle, or the end of the story. Then the rest of the class incorporates that idea in a class or individual story.

MARLEE (age 9): One day as I was collecting wood for our campfire, I heard a strange sound. (opening sentence)
NINA (age 6): The salamander had nothing to eat. (middle of the story)
DAN (age 7): We were glad to see the end of that day. (end sentence)

Retelling a story

Overheard snatches of conversation make good story starters. I introduce one I heard recently as an example of permitted eavesdropping:

Two girls were running frantically down the sidewalk. One shouted, "Stacey's been arrested for shoplifting in Overwaitea. Come on."

Concerned students ask, "What did they look like? Is it for real?"

I suggest they create a story or drama about what happened before the girls get there, and what happens when they arrive.

We retell stories frequently. I introduce the retelling technique something like this. I ask students to think of something really lucky or unlucky that has happened to them, or an adventure, or a funny incident, or something strange and spooky. Then each student tells the incident to someone in the class. Each is asked to talk in turn and listen carefully to the partner's story. Then each student moves on to another student to retell the story just heard. In this way students begin to appreciate that this is what storytelling is all about — the telling of one's own and other people's stories.

After telling a story, I ask the class to retell it, a little bit at a time around the circle, and to tell it in their own words. Often I hand around the object I used during my telling. In the story "The Big Tree and the Little Tree," for example, I pass a pine branch around the circle. For a retelling of "The Princess on the Glass Mountain," in which the Witch of Darkness changes the princess into a bird, I pass around a small wooden bird.

For a class of ESL children (ages 6-7) I tell the story of Raintaro, a little known legend from Japan, based on the picture book of the same name by Toshiko Kanzwa (Gakken, 1972). The content is very similar to "Crow Boy" by Yashima Taro, where an orphan boy is finally accepted into the community.

"Raintaro," which I narrate in language a little more formal than everyday use and in which I include several Japanese names, customs, and phrases, is about an old washerwoman.

RAINTARO

One night during a rainstorm an old washerwoman hears crying in the wind. She follows the sound and finds a baby boy sitting on a rock in the river. She takes him home and cares for him, and tells him that the Raindragon who lives high up on the mountain overlooking the village must have sent him to her, because she was lonely. She believes the Raindragon is Raintaro's father. This frightens the child, who is already scared of everyone in the village. Even the frogs make him cry. Of course all the other children tease him and call him crybaby.

A drought comes to the village, crops die, the beautiful river turns to mud, and the old woman becomes sick. She tells the boy of her longing for a drink of clear water.

Raintaro bravely sets off up the mountain, and though terrified of the dark and the height, and of the dragon himself, he perseveres, meets his father the Raindragon, and brings back the rain. And so Raintaro saves the village.

Corey (age 7) and three partners dramatize the story like this, very much encapsulating the plot!

OLD WOMAN:	I wish I had a boy.
BOY:	The boy cried in the pond.
OLD WOMAN:	Here is some food.
BOY:	Thanks.
OLD WOMAN:	There is no water.
BOY:	I will get water for you.
OLD WOMAN:	Here is a cake to take.
BOY:	There is a rabbit.
RABBIT:	I know where the water is.
BOY:	Where?
RABBIT:	Up here, boy. Look at it.
DRAGON:	What do you want?
BOY:	Some water.
DRAGON:	Okay, you may have water.
BOY:	I am going home.
OLD WOMAN:	We have water.

Later, Corey drew a picture which shows the boy in native Indian dress.

Updating stories

Groups of three, four, or five choose a familiar story, such as "Goldilocks and the Three Bears," "Hansel and Gretel," or "The Fisherman and His Wife," or even a nursery rhyme. They then find a way of retelling or modernizing the story. I often read students sections of Roald Dahl's

Revolting Rhymes (Bantam Skylark, 1986) to illustrate inventions on a familiar theme.

Matching stories to their settings

We tell stories set in locations chosen by the group: a haunted house, a deserted island, an isolated street, a restaurant. When the location has been chosen, students must find a dramatic incident that could occur there.

A group of Grade 9 students chose a bus depot. In the Depression years on Christmas Eve a runaway is returning home. The last bus to the boy's home is delayed by a snowstorm. The story is told in flashback style, telling of the boy's leaving home and his determination to find work. In his pocket is his final month's pay. He's afraid he won't get home in time to make it a good Christmas.

Finding stories in place names

Sometimes we look up place names and devise the story of how the place might have got its name: Sister Mountain, Gold River, Alert Bay, Moose Jaw, Kicking Horse Pass, Camper Creek, Shelter Bay, Bonanza Creek, Dunk River, Blow Me Down, Black Joke Cove. The stories are often as melodramatic as the incidents that must have originated the names in the first place.

The following place name story was composed by two Grade 10 students, Leslie and Laurie.

THE EIGHT SISTERS

At one time the popular mountains called "The Seven Sisters" had an eighth sister that had passed away many years ago. Most people haven't heard about this, but we have proof that there once was an eighth sister. To prove this theory we walked by foot to the peak to find evidence of her existence. The moment after we arrived at the top we had found a mountain known as the "Queen's Face." We had found out that the "Queen's Face" just happens to be the mother of the eight sisters. Hours after mountain walking, we discovered the grave of the eighth sister, which was made of stone.

Adding details

A favorite class story-making technique is to go around the story circle three times, saying one word on the first round, two words on the next, then three and four on the last.

An excellent concentration device, because it involves counting words as well as adding details, is to build the number of words consecutively to ten and then start back at one. For example,

1. Once
2. I saw
3. a large green
4. snake. It was slithering
5. down the rock face which
6. I was trying to climb because
7. my best friend was trapped half way
8. up the mountain. He had got stuck and
9. was unable to move. I reached up, held out
10. my glove, hoping to distract the venomous poison snake, but

1. it
2. was hopeless.
3. Suddenly a rock . . . .

and so on.

Performing a story

Students are asked to imagine that they have been invited to perform a story for a special group of people. I suggest:

— senior citizens on a winter afternoon at their community centre

- children at a birthday party (the magician cancelled at the last minute and the children will be disappointed)
- teenage campers at their final campfire in a remote part of a national park
- students on an exchange visit from another country a children's hospital
- a neighborhood Hallowe'en party

We talk about the importance and effect of the setting, the circumstances surrounding the event itself, and how to choose material for a specific audience. (Bob Barton's *Tell Me Another*, Chapter 2, has an excellent chart showing what a storyteller might keep in mind when matching stories and audiences. See the Selected Bibliography.)

Some stories appeal to a wide range of ages and interests; in fact, ''a good story is a good story for everyone,'' as Bob Barton notes. The class offers examples of universally loved favorites, as well as ideas for stories which might be suitable only for a particular group, in a particular space, or at a particular time.

Students decide which group they would like to perform for. They then agree to work individually or with one or more storytellers. The prepared stories vary from retellings of familiar tales and reworkings of class efforts to brand new ones. The planning and rehearsing take up more than one session.

The class acts as an audience in an appropriate way, helping to create a secure atmosphere for the storytellers. The group is discouraged from acting the part of anything but good listeners, never attempting to become 'old people' or 'tiny children'. The occasion is an exercise in sharing and performance.

Student storytellers are encouraged to select their own lighting effects as much as possible: daylight, electric light, semi-darkness, even candlelight to enhance the atmosphere.

6

A letter is a story

Letters are stories. We discuss the kinds of letters students write, from invitations and thank-you notes to important, meaningful tellings of personal experiences. We work on both existing and new letters, always searching for and discussing the story within.

Helen (age 9) writes to a newspaper:

Dear Sir,
We found a bird today. The cat next door bit it. I thought it was hurt badly, so we took it in. We put it in a box, so the cat could not get it. It was lying down with a warm cloth over it in the front hall. Then the bird died. All cats should have bells on their collars. I think there should be a law that cats need bells.

Helen

Jason (age 11) writes to his father:

Dear Dad,
I wish you would stop smoking, like Mum, and could be home more often. Dad, there's something I've always wanted to say to you. You know how you get mad and yell? Well, I feel like killing you, but I soon get over my anger and forgive you. You

know those things you buy me like records and little stuff, it's not necessary, but thanks anyway.

Love, Jason

Students quickly realize that there is usually an urgent reason behind the letter, the kind of urgency that creates stories.

Completing mystery letters

I explain that the portion of the letters they are going to read or hear is all that remains of the original letter. They are to fill in the missing bits, rearranging the information in any way they like and completing the letter in their own words. They are to tell us about the person who wrote it and clarify the problem or resolve the conflict.

In groups of two, three or four, students brainstorm how they can best tell the story in letter form from the meagre clues typed at random on the sheet.

Here are three samples *before* completion!

For a Grade 8, 9 or 10 group:

_____

_____

April 2, 1901

Dear _____:
I have no one else to turn to, so I hope and pray you can help us. _____

_____

I am 18 years old with a young child. _____

_____

_____ last three months _____

work _____ so hungry.

_____

Yours respectfully,

_____

For a Grade 5/6 class:

Crescent Camp

August 5, _____

Dear Mum,
When I left _____
_____ I thought _____ howling _____
to a wolf den _____
I'm tired _____ dream _____
always somewhere _____
_____ coming home.

Love,

_____

For a Grade 7 class:

_____

_____

_____

Hi,
You'll never believe the _____
_____ great excitement.
When can _____
This place is _____
_____
_____

Bye for now,

_____

In the following completed letter by two Grade 9 girls the directing words have been italicized and the location omitted:

April 2, 1901

Dear Aunt and Uncle,
When I said farewell to my parents in England almost a year ago now, I little thought I would need to burden you with my problems. My poor parents, if they only knew it, are grandparents, yes, of a lovely baby boy now six weeks old. Alas, his father never saw him. When the blizzard raged for three weeks, he tried to get help for me. I begged him not to go out. He did not even reach our neighbors. We found his body ten days later, frozen, three feet from the animal shed. I found your address among his papers. *I have no one else to turn to.* We do not own the farm, *so I hope and pray you can help us. I am 18 years old with a young child*, and must find *work* or we will both starve. The baby is always *so hungry*. Please reply soon.

Respectfully,
Your niece, Anna

The completed letters are often an excellent starting point for dramatic interpretation, as clear clues for characterization and a strong narrative line are usually present.

The above letter was dramatized with a narrator telling the story in flashback while the letter was read. The scene of Anna about to give birth and begging her husband not to leave her, the long wait, and the final search and finding of the body were movingly told. The saga of Anna could have gone on. There was her whole future to tell stories about and potential for research on women in the prairies in the early 1900s.

Answering letters

Students reply to a letter, orally or in writing, assuming the character's voice as much as possible. A student, writing in role as a parent, answers Jason's accusations. Anna's relatives respond warmly or negatively for various reasons for her pleas for help. Pet owners write to the editor of their local newspaper regarding the pros and cons of wearing warning bells.

Fairy tale characters write letters to their families or friends. Cinderella writes a letter to her fairy godmother telling her about life in the palace; Hans writes to his father on a scrap of paper while being fattened in the witch's cage.

This is Megan (age 8) writing to Mother Pig, telling her of her plight after leaving home. She writes in character as one of the Three Little Pigs.

Dear Mum,
This week has been a disaster. The Big Bad Wolf chased us on Tuesday afternoon, and huff and puff *down* went Billy's house. On Wednesday we had to clean up Billy's house. On Thursday he huffed and puffed again, and blew down Ryan's house. And now he's blowing on *my* house and still going strong.

Your loving Little Pig,
Megan

Interpreting and dramatizing letters

Stories and novels often contain letters that are reference points for further storytelling potential. Sarah Elizabeth Wheaton's response to Jacob Whiting's advertisement for a wife can inspire students to write and respond to real or imagined advertisements in the personal columns of the local newspaper. (Patricia MacLachlan. *Sarah Plain and Tall*. New York: Harper and Row, 1985)

Students then choose which advertisements to reply to in character, and the interview is dramatized. Sarah's letter also leads to discussion and scenes of farewell. Students dramatize their own scenes (or those of characters in stories) of saying goodbye to one group of people and one way of life before embarking on another and having to become part of a new group. Sarah's letter hints strongly at her reasons for agreeing to travel so far from home: her brother William's forthcoming marriage. Students are eager to explore the potential drama in such a situation, for example, the first meeting between Sarah and her prospective sister-in-law; or perhaps William's attempts to persuade her to stay on. Would Sarah discuss her choices with a best friend? More stories always lie just under the surface, offering many dramatic routes to investigate.

Kit Pearson's *The Sky Is Falling* (Penguin, 1991) is the story of a British evacuee and her younger brother, and their efforts to accept and become part of their new Canadian family in Toronto during the 1939-45 wartime.

Ben Wick's *No Time to Say Goodbye* (Stoddart, 1988) contains numerous letters written by children age 4-15 during those wartime years, each one a source for story and drama. Many speak of harsh and poignant times; the children experience hunger, cruelty, bullying, as well as fun, laughter and caring. Because the letters are true, and each is written with a different voice, they make a strong basis for dramatic exploration suitable for a wide age group.

7

Stories inside stories

Inside each story is another story and still another. What happens to the person who helps the heroine on her quest? Where is the story about the other people she has helped or not, depending on the circumstances? Do Cinderella and her prince live happily ever after, or must the fairy godmother return and solve another problem? What happens to the Ugly Sisters? Do they have a change of heart? Unlikely! We know the Ugly Duckling turns into a beautiful young swan. Is that it? What of his new life? What does Goldilocks find the next time she walks into the woods?

In Michael Morpurgo's *Little Foxes* (Mammoth, 1990), Billy is an orphan who came in a box labeled 'Perishable' and was delivered to the local police station, but that's all we know. We find out about his life at ten, how he runs away and finds a happy home on a barge helping to save wild life, and then nothing more. What happened before and what happens after? This is the source for many new stories, especially when characters are already strongly established.

Thinking about 'before' and 'after'

Poems hold a wealth of untapped stories. In Theodore Roethke's ''Meadow Mouse,'' the poet feeds the small creature three different kinds of cheese and beds it snugly in a shoebox on the back porch. Yet, the next morning the box is empty. What brought the mouse to him? Does it get home safely? What further adventure lie in store in the wild countryside? What happened before the story in the poem begins and what happens after it ends?

Dionne Brand's poem "The Bottleman" appears in her book *Earth Magic* (Kids Can Press, 1979). Many questions for new stories are posed within the poem.

The Bottleman

"bottles! bottles!"
hear the bottleman's cry,
"empty bottles! old bottles!
bottles with corks! bottles without!"
his wheel barrow finds every rut in the street,
his sharp eyes search every spot.
there, in a ditch,
a dirty green bottle,
a treasure, a precious jewel,
an exquisite emerald in his mind.
where is he going?
from where does he come?
barrow trundling through the streets,
crying
"bottles! empty bottles"
treasures in a bottleman's dreams.

We read the poem aloud and talk about it. Here are some questions for new stories:

Where is the bottleman going?
From where does he come?
Why does he collect bottles?
What dream is he searching for?
What happens when he finds his dream?

Designing a story space

We start by collecting bottles of many different varieties. When we have enough, so that there is one bottle for each participant, we begin a design in the middle of the story circle. Bright sunlight is ideal. A sense of mystery is created if we set our design in a darkened room illuminated by candlelight or flashlights. The design takes a while to complete, and each student must be careful not to disturb the arrangement made by the previous person. When the last bottle is in place, we walk around and look at the design from every possible angle, standing and looking down, even trying to look up, from a distance, and close by. We talk about our immediate impressions. It looks like —

- a junkyard
- a space station
- a city of the future
- a hall of mirrors in a fairground
- an underwater civilization
- a valuable collection in an antique store
- a ghost town
- a germ free, pollution free city

I ask, "What happens there?" Students group together, working on ideas that deliberately conflict or that they agree upon.

I remind them that we are interested in three questions:
WHO? Who are the people who live, used to live, or will live in this space?
WHY? Why is the space there?
WHAT? What happens there and what is the secret contained within those walls or in that space?

Roger (age 9) begins his story this way:
I have invented a time machine. I'm off to the future. I have gone past the Big Dipper. Now I have gone past the Milky Way. I have landed in the future. Everything here runs on air. . . .

Peter (age 10) begins:

There was a great white light, and a shadowed figure in the blinding light. It called in an ominous voice: "Do you really want to go to the future?"

"There's a message in the bottle."

I choose a medium-size bottle of dark green glass, the neck large enough for a piece of paper to be slid inside. Each student is asked to print a message to go in the bottle, the sentence to give a clue to the reader of the kind of help that might be required and some indication as to who wrote it in the first place. The temptation, of course, is just to write "HELP!"

We sit in a circle, and I ask a student to draw a message from the bottle. (Names on the other side of the paper help me ensure that students don't get their own message back.) A volunteer reads the message dramatically: "Help! I am a good genie trapped by an evil magician. Follow the bank of the river to the large oak and . . . ." The message is handed to the next student who continues the story for a short while, with the voice of the finder, before passing the story on.

Four students respond:

- I don't know whether to believe the message or not. It might be my mean brother trying to trick me again.
- I decide to risk it. Suddenly a hawk circles around my head.
- Is he trying to tell me something?
- It seems to want me to follow it.

A Grade 8 student writes:

Whoever finds this bottle and reads this message may be too late. I am stranded in shark-infested waters. My boat capsized off the coast of Tasmania. I know there is someone on the island, because I have heard strange sounds of drum beats and howls in the night. Help me, please!

A Grade 4/5 student writes:

Please find me. I am trapped in a cabin in the woods outside of town. I am hungry. I tied this bottle to my dog's collar. He will show you the way.

Students also enjoy solving the story of their own message before handing it over to a partner. A time limit of five minutes or so is given. Then each partner exchanges stories based on the same message. Collaborations of small groups often lend themselves to dramatic scenes. I request that the final drama clearly show the events leading up to the writing of the message, who sends it, who finds it, and how the problem is solved, or if not, why not.

8

In the news

Newspapers and magazines are powerful sources for story building.

Making newspaper objects

As a warm-up activity, I give each student part of a newspaper from which to make an object. These range in scope from balls to hats, swords, boats, a fan, a kite, a lace tablecloth, a footprint, an apron, a cloak, a fish, a bowl. Even the youngest children 'see' an image or shape in a crumpled sheet of newspaper.

I group students into fours or fives, arbitrarily, so that they have no choice over which newspaper objects go together. Sometimes the objects are first identified around the story circle, and the participants select which props, and thus potential group members, go together. This might result in a ball, a telescope, a tree and a boat in the same group. A story is created which includes everyone's object in a meaningful way!

More difficult is a story circle with the entire class, each person having to incorporate the object into the story. This is a warm-up that taxes even the most creative group.

We explore news headlines by first creating our own around the story circle: CHILD FOUND IN BUSH. FIRE. BEAR

HUNTS HUNTER. We choose one from many efforts. Then a volunteer 'reads' (speaks out loud) the story that might accompany the headline.

Bringing the news to life

Students work in small groups to make up an original headline. They create the photograph that goes with the news story, using their bodies in a frozen picture before coming to life as narrators to tell the story. For example, "A twelve-year-old boy was swept away by a swift current in the River Nicomekl. His dog Lad jumped in and held on to him until help arrived."

We do 'Before and After' stories, telling about events that lead up to the moment the picture and news occur and what happens after all the publicity has died down.

Often these ideas are linked to real events. Students are asked to search magazines and newspapers for pictures, headlines, and stories that will yield new stories for us to tell.

Here is one that they found:

MURKA is a Moscow cat, who has twice attacked and killed a family canary. Her punishment is banishment to Voronezh, to live with the children's grandmother. Months later she returns to her old neighborhood, minus the tip of her tail and with a torn ear.

What happened to her? What adventures did she have before coming home?

Making up what might have happened

A Grade 5/6 class looks up the distance between Moscow and Voronezh. They are hundreds of kilometres apart. Maybe the cat never reached Voronezh at all.

Many class ideas later, one group describes what might have happened:

Dad says, "We have to get rid of that cat. I warned you the last time this happened. She's a menace!"

Luckily, Grandmother was staying with them at the time. She said, "I'll tell you what. I'll take her back home with me. She can catch mice instead of canaries, and one day she may learn her lesson. Find me a basket with a lid."

The whole family go with Murka and Grandmother to the bus depot where they wave and wave till the bus is out of sight.

The moment the bus halts for a rest stop, Murka pushes open the lid of her basket and climbs out. Grandmother is fast asleep. The bus driver has gone out for coffee, and Murka sneaks into his lunch box under the driver's seat. She eats a piece of sausage and goes to sleep too. When Grandmother arrives home and finds the empty basket, she thinks maybe that's a good solution. She phones the family and tells them. The children never give up hope that one day they may get Murka back.

The bus driver lives in Moscow, in a street far away from Murka's neighborhood. When the driver's wife opens the lunch box to wash it, she screams. Murka is scared and jumps out the kitchen window. She lands in the back alley and hides behind a garbage can where she stays until dark. Then she comes out and starts looking for food. The alley cats see that she's a stranger and well cared for. They spit and hiss and scratch, "Fat cat! Rich cat! This is our place." Murka is cornered. They start to fight and make a lot of noise. Murka is hurt. One cat bites her ear, another her tail. A waiter from a restaurant comes out to check on the noise and rescues Murka. He keeps her in the restaurant kitchen to catch mice and rats.

One day the waiter lets his little boy come to supper with him. Peter sees Murka and pleads to keep her. "All right, she can be your birthday present." Murka likes Peter, just about as much as she did the kids who owned her before. One day the teacher in Peter's class asks them to write about their pets. When Peter reads about Murka, Anna recognizes her own cat from the description. She tells her brother at playtime.

Rudi, who is in the next grade, says, "Listen, we think you've got our cat."

Peter is very upset and angry. "Anyone can say that. She's my birthday present. You think my father stole her?" He's ready for a fight.

At that moment the bell rings and the other kids line up. Peter and Rudi are yelling at each other, "Thief!" "Liar!" They get sent to the principal's office. The principal phones the boys' parents.

Peter's dad thinks maybe Max, who is really Murka, could be the family's cat. Peter, his parents, and Max/Murka go to visit the family's apartment. There is even a photograph of Murka with Rudi and Anna.

Anna has a great idea to solve the problem: "Let's share her. You get her for one month, and we get her for one month." The parents agree, and Peter says, "You can have her first."

A Grade 4 class decides to work out some of the ways Murka escapes from various situations: she climbs roofs, swims through sewers and almost drowns.

Dramatizing the story

I suggest that the story may be divided into chapter headings. These then become the titles of the scenes for a class play. The class has agreed that we can incorporate many of each group's ideas.

They decide on the following scenes:

1. Get rid of that cat.
2. Murka escapes.
3. Alley cats.
4. Rescue.
5. School.

6. The fight.
7. The principal's office.
8. Sharing Murka.

The class divides into groups, each one taking responsibility for a particular scene.

What follows is a portion of the dialogue when Murka is discovered after the canary's chase, fall, and accidental death:

ANNA: Please let her stay. Just give her one more chance.
DAD: She's had her chance. Don't you care about the bird?
RUDI: She's only young. She'll learn.
DAD: She's going! That's my last word!

The play was performed in sequence, each group taking the spotlight in turn, with the rest of the class as audience — a method that allows for multicasting. The entire sequence lasted three sessions.

A headline is found about a young boy missing from home for two days before being brought in by the police. The boy said, "I just had a bad day." Vivid stories and dramatizations of what the bad day was really like are immediately forthcoming: a bad report card, a sick pet who had to be put down, a sick pet who had to be put down, fights with friends and siblings, teasing by a playground bully.

I ask one class to imagine each of them (as the boy), confiding to a friend their intention to run away, and why.

Jennifer (age 11) tells her story:

I hate mornings. I always get off to a bad start. I get dressed quickly before I freeze to death just because my dad insists on turning the heat way down to save money. Today I got off to a bad start as usual. At breakfast my disgusting sister is spitting grapefruit seeds at me. Mum yells at *me*: "Clear the table, load the dishwasher, feed the dog, make your bed, and don't forget to lock the door,

Bye, have a good day. I'll be back at five. Oh, and make some supper. Just make anything!"
I won't be there. I'm running away.

Improvisation based on a news item

A Grade 10 drama group improvises the story behind the headline of an elderly, homeless man who finds a fortune of $29,000 and turns it over to the police. The money is the life savings of an elderly woman.

The students use the prop box to help build the characters. One group selects a battered gray trilby from the hat box, and works out a story. Each student assumes the role of the street person and tells an imaginary TV reporter about his or her life:

St. 1: So, you'd like to know something about me. I guess you could say I'm just an ordinary person.

[The hat is passed on.]

St. 2: I left school in Grade 10, got a good job fixing bikes. When I was 20 I got married and had a couple of kids.

St. 3: Joined the army and went to Korea. They don't tell you what it feels like to kill a man. All that marching wrecked my feet.

St. 4: Look at me now. I'm a pretty good walker, wouldn't you say? Just walking the sidewalks.

St. 5: My wife died. I couldn't take care of the kids. Welfare took them and put them in a home. Haven't seen them in a long time. Got families of their own now, I guess.

St. 1: I just couldn't take it, losing them, I mean. Quit my job, quit my town, and moved on.

St. 2: Times is tough. Got bronchitis [student coughs], no insurance, just coughed my way from job to job.

St. 3: Got laid off. Rents is high. Got me a tent, picked up my radio. I go where I please.

In the role of TV reporter I ask, "Weren't you tempted to keep the money?"

St. 4: I guess for a while there. I thought about it. It would be stealing, though, wouldn't it?

St. 5: Couldn't sleep nights if I did that. Anyways, got no place to keep that kind of money.

St. 1: Buy some smokes. That's how I found it, looking for butts in a trash can.

Students in pairs improvise the possible dialogue between the man and the woman, each one switching roles in turn. Some future soap operas result.

On average I find at least three possible news stories a week. "Some farmers in a remote European village reported seeing three-eyed extra-terrestrials land, and are worried about the milk delivery. The local driver is now afraid he will be captured by the thirsty humanoids." Exciting escape stories abound. "Two young Romanian boys were forced to work as spies for the secret police and then tried to save some orphan children."

Students like to bring in their own news items. Recently a report about a 12-year-old-girl who was put off the bus on an isolated stretch of road, because of abrupt changes to the route, provoked anguished commentaries. We dramatized:

— the girl speaking her own thoughts aloud as she watched the bus lights disappear
— the girl asking help from strangers (each student asking in a different way).

Then we retold fairy tales and myths about abandoned children. The students recall their personal memories.

The class built a one-word-each story about being lost. The group shared an experience common to each of them: the five-year-old's feeling of fear and confusion when lost momentarily in a large store or mall. Each student froze into an image (or still picture) of the emotion felt on 'being lost'. The tableau is akin to a photograph which captures a moment of joy or panic. Then each student emerged from this tableau of frozen time and spoke the single word that would represent the theme.

The following was produced rapidly by the group and was then dramatized:

Once
I
was
lost
in
a
supermarket.
I
was
very
scared.
Then
my
mother
found
me.
She
was
happy.
I
was
glad.
She
said,
"Never
get
lost
again."
I
never
did.

Lisa (13), generously shared a personal experience with the group about her feelings of abandonment:

I'm telling you this story because I think kids in my place should know that there is a way to find out about who your real mother is. When I was 10 weeks old, the family I'm living with right now took me as their child. I never found out about my mother. I cried at night thinking my real mother didn't love me. Then I read about a mother who told the newspaper that she had a good reason why she gave up her son, and what that lady said really helped me about my mother. Some kids don't even have a mother or father. When I'm older I will be able to look up my real mother in the hospital records if I want to.

This particular story, told anonymously to different groups, tied in with various 'foundling' stories that had been researched in newspapers and prompted new stories, often dramatized, of searches, disappointments, confrontations, and reunions. These new stories had their roots in real life drama.

Students enjoy creating their own newspaper sections, working as reporters, editors, and photographers to build stories for Family, Youth, World, or Local news sections.

The idea of a press deadline appeals. I assign various slots that must be filled on the spot. Two students may be given five or ten minutes to come up with a story for the Sports section; another group must report on an imaginary meeting on the environment, or the election speech of a candidate for a new political party. Everyone enjoys the practice in spontaneity and an opportunity to try out different voices and characters under 'pressure'.

What happens when a headline story is over? How do people go back to living ordinary lives after being a hero or a victim for hours or days? What is the story we are not told? This is an area of investigation with many possibilities.

The newspaper is a rich and endless source for dramatic narrative.

9

Something from long ago — a drama

Each student in a group of 9-to-11-year-olds is asked to bring to class an object, photo or piece of information to help us create the plot of a movie or play about something that happened long ago.

Students return to class with a fantastic variety of objects: old or outdated Valentine's Day cards, photos, lace, samplers, ancient teddy bears, old school readers, china ornaments, a brooch, a brass candlestick, a carpet beater, a washboard, an old wooden cooking spoon, coins, a piece of flint, a walking stick, and a handmade quilt.

Telling the history of the treasures

The students speak about their treasures: who it belongs to, its approximate age, and provide any special information they have about it. A wealth of possible stories emerges, but there is no doubt which article captures everyone's imagination: Zoe has brought in her great grandfather's lunch pail. None of us has ever seen one like this: an intricate arrangement of stacked tins of different shapes and sizes all fitting together neatly like a jigsaw puzzle. Smooth to touch and burnished by age.

The emerging story

ZOE: This is the lunch pail my great grandfather used when he was a miner.

ULYSSE: (An 11-year-old recent arrival from Spain) I think the story is about a boy who wants to be a farmer, but he must work in the mine instead.

ALEXIS: Yes, and he finds gold in the mine and so he gets enough money to be a farmer.

GILLY: There is an accident in the mine, but after a long time he finds the way out and he finds himself far away in another town, and gets adopted by a rich farmer.

ME: So everyone agrees that the story should happen a long time ago?

AMBER: About a hundred years ago.

ME: How does the lunch pail play an important part in the story?

JOEL: It's his first day at work, and his mother gives him the lunch bucket to take down the mine.

ALLYSON: He loves horses. That's what he wants to do, work with horses, but the family is too poor.

RYAN: And he has to be a miner like his dad.

ME: Do his parents understand how he feels about working underground?

ZOE: Yes, and his mother put a big piece of cake with his bread and cheese, because it's his first day.

ULYSSE: He's 13 years old and sad to leave school.

ME: Let's set up the classroom on his last day in school and find out what it was like then.

Back in time: class and teacher in role

Within a short time the students have arranged chairs in rows and decide that they want to have a very strict teacher. They discuss the kind of school work they would have to do, and we improvise chanting various times tables, passing notes in class, the games that are played in the schoolyard, and the disciplined kind of behavior expected in class. Joel wants to be a boy who is always late. I need to return them to the basic story we have begun.

ME (in role as the teacher, Mrs. Mckenzie): Today, class, the last day before the holidays, I want each of you to tell us about your ambition when you graduate. When I point to you, stand up and say your name clearly so I can mark you off on the register.

The group takes on various roles, and makes up new names. They enjoy this piece of drama immensely. What emerges is that the story will take place in a poor mining village and that Tom (Zoe's grandfather's name was Thomas) hates what he hears of the mine from the bigger boys. He does not like the dark; instead he wants to work in the open air with animals.

This story continues over several sessions, and the class dramatizes various group scenes, such as the supper where Tom tells his parents how he feels about going down the mine. The class is divided into different groups of their own choosing for this family scene. The families vary in size, and they either show what happens in their scene (for example, the family reaction to Tom's confession) or talk about it.

We also set up the mine and work without sight or very little light to simulate the darkness there. The group demands a cave-in, which they improvise at some length, using tables to create tunnels. They decide that Tom has a candlestick and matches with him (one of the students has brought in an old box of wooden matches) so that he can light this when he is very frightened.

This disaster becomes the highlight of the story. Students are very involved with Tom because it is his story. At this time, the plight of the other miners is not gone into very deeply, except that some are injured, or die, and many are rescued.

MELISSA:	Tom is separated from the others. He calls and calls, but there is no answer.
NATHAN:	Because there was so much fallen rock.
JOEL:	He walks about for days, looking for a way out.
ALLYSON:	He still has some bread left in his lunch pail, and this saves his life.
GILLY:	His candle stub gets smaller and smaller.
AMBER:	There is no air and he can't shout any more.
ULYSSE:	He thinks he is going to die.
ALEXIS:	He hears water rushing. He is so thirsty that he tries to reach it.
ASHLEY:	He pushes and pushes against the rock, and at last it gives way.
ALEXIS:	The water had softened the rock. It was another way out of the mine.
GILLY:	He pushes up through the water, and suddenly he's in a field. He lies there.
ASHLEY:	Something cold licks his face. It's a pony.
NATHAN:	He didn't know where he was. Then someone was shaking him and asking, "Who are you?"
STACEY:	It was the farmer who owned the field.
ALLYSON:	He lets Tom stay with him and learn about horses.
ME:	What happened to his family?
ULYSSE:	The farmer lets him ride home to tell them he was safe, and he later becomes a farmer.

The process

The bringing in of the objects, the discussion, and the improvisation to the final happy ending take four sessions.

We are able to incorporate several other students' objects into the story. One family group has the mother stir the cake mixture with the wooden spoon; the old school reader is worked in to the classroom scene, and of course the candle and matches become significant details.

In this instance the drama happens concurrently, and sometimes precedes the story. The whole experience becomes important and vivid to the students. Follow-up work includes both oral and written retelling of the drama/story.

Students are eager to describe how they feel at different moments of crisis in the story:

— not being able to follow their real inclinations because of family demands;
— being underground for the first time (we simulated going down the 'cage' to the mine);
— how it feels to be alone in the dark after the accident;
— the comfort brought by the last piece of cake or bread in the lunch pail;
— reaching safety and light.

For Ulysse in particular, this story-making episode brings out strong contributions and involvement. Alexis (9), who originally suggests that the boy should discover gold in the mine, happily goes along with the class story.

10

Mixed bag

Footprints

The students and I gather around a large, previously cut out, paper footprint taped to the floor. I tell them that this is a simulated footprint of a living dinosaur.

In role as fellow scientist, I ask them how they would feel about capturing a creature that size. From the size and shape of the footprint (approximate size one metre or three feet), could they conjecture any opinion about the possible appearance of the creature?

I then read a letter addressed to us from The International Society of Cryptozoology. This contains an invitation to do preliminary research and exploration on the reported existence of Mokele-Mbembe, also known as Mackal. Our findings will be submitted at the next meeting of the society. Mackal is believed to live in a swampy part of the Congo, which remains largely unexplored.

The letter is discussed.

Students in pairs are asked to compile a list of equipment that would be necessary for such an expedition.

We talk about the importance of trying to interview local residents who may have heard, sighted, or had experience with the dinosaur. Imaginary interviews are conducted in pairs and threes, each student in turn taking on the role of local villager and of scientist.

Students group themselves and discuss their findings. Together each group of five or six arrives at a final description of Mackal and then reports back to the whole class.

By this time the footprint has become as much a reality for us as the dinosaur.

(In the early 80s the International Society of Cryptozoology, which is based in Chicago, actually did set out for deepest Africa armed with sonar devices, video cameras, and old-fashioned nets to look for the creature.)

We are now ready to tell our stories about Mackal either in groups or around the story circle. We can speak as:

— scientists who have heard stories about the creature
— villagers who have invested the dinosaur with special powers, who are telling the scientists about the creature
— ourselves, wanting to tell a story about the last representative of a bygone age.

For younger audiences (Kindergarten – Grade 2), I gather the students around the footprint and speak very quietly;

ME: I found this when I came in today. Perhaps we'd better not touch it. Can you think of a reason?
STUDENT: Because it's old.
STUDENT: It's poison.
STUDENT: It's a paper egg.
STUDENT: It's magic.
ME: And suppose it crumbles away?
STUDENT: It looks like an elephant's foot.
ME: Where did it come from?
STUDENT: The window.
STUDENT: Under the carpet.
STUDENT: Under the floorboards.
ME: When did it get here?
STUDENT: It came in the night, in the dark.
ME: What's it looking for?
STUDENT: Erasers.
ME: Let's start the story.

(Amid much laughter, hands shoot up, everyone wanting to begin.)

BEN: Once upon a time a monster lived in a school.
JAY: Under the floorboards.
JANET: It's favorite food was erasers.
ME: Any kind, any color — but one day. . .

The story continues.

Color stories

How colors make one feel is a favorite topic with children.
SHERI (age 10): Black makes me feel mad and angry. Yellow and orange make me feel loving towards people.
   Groups describe the many aspects of one color and layers of meaning emerge. Ashley, Janet, Jacki, and Gillian (ages 10-13) respond:

• Orange is an orange blossom at a wedding.
• It's the sun setting behind the mountains.
• It's the glow of the campfire.
• It's the big poppy in the cornfield.
• It's a beach ball, a sunshade, a glass of juice.
• It's an orange.

   Pairs or groups select contrasting colors and create a scene that reflects their images and ideas. They try to incorporate the mood and emotion of the colors into the telling.

Something out of place

Students look for the unexpected in a landscape. We walk with paper and felt pen. Anything that seems incongruous is drawn or noted: a juggler in a shopping mall, an old sneaker on a curb, a coin on a woodland path. Whatever is out of place becomes the focus of a story.

Theatre sets (shoebox design)

Students design imaginary movie or stage sets inside a shoebox. The box may be made up sparsely, or it may be crowded with colors and effects, using any junk materials, modeling clay or figures that are available.

We choose one of the boxes and groups are asked to imagine themselves as characters within the set.

They build a story of what they might be doing there, who they are, and what they want. Then they bring the scene to life through dramatization.

Spaces/places

Large, interesting outlines are drawn on full sheets of construction paper and distributed one per group of four or five students. The outline is like a featureless map.

Each group now interprets its map:

• a treasure map
• underground caves
• an archaeological dig
• a deserted tropical island
• the site of a research centre

It takes time for agreement to be established. Before the 'map' can be illustrated the students must decide:

Who they are: spies, refugees, scientists, explorers, film crew.

What their relationship is to the document, and why it has significance for them — perhaps, also, what they are willing to go through to retain it.

Whether they are about to embark on a journey or are simply documenting discoveries already made. They may be dealing with stolen plans, or they may be in the process of designing something, or decoding, or chartering a voyage.

What difficulties and obstacles they face.

No suggestions are given, each group being responsible for its own decisions. As discussion proceeds, the 'map' may be filled in with felt markers. A question arises: Is the group documenting one experience only, or might individuals have separate stories to tell? For example, if the project involves underground caves, the explorers could get separated and experience different adventures.

This is a lengthy project and may take several sessions. When each group has completed its task, the stories are shared with the class. Although the stories are oral, they frequently spill over into writing and art, not only on the original outline but within each project in the guise of messages, reports, and journals.

Pictures, artcards, sculptures, photographs

Students express the dialogue or thoughts of the subject at the moment the picture was created. This dialogue may become the basis of an improvisation. Consider, for example, the picture of a little girl peering longingly through some railings in Monet's *Gare Saint-Lazare* (National Gallery of Art, Washington). Why must she stay outside? Is the young woman with her a sister, an aunt, a nanny, her mother?

What is the secret expedition in Lowry's *The Pond* (Detail, 1950, Tate Gallery, London)? Where are they going? What is printed on their banners?

Is the mother in Picasso's *La Mere* (City Art Museum, St. Louis, Missouri) thinking of the past or the future? What are her thoughts? Students, in role as mother or child, express those thoughts, or dramatize the 'before' and 'after' of the picture.

Using make-up to stimulate story

Students in pairs or threes are given a choice of two or three face make-up sticks. They then take turns making up each other as a character: human, fantasy, animal, or spirit. After the masks are finished, the students discuss the results and how they feel about them.

All instructions and suggestions are given one step at a time. Students are encouraged to take their time; obviously not everyone will be finished simultaneously.

Next, the pairs begin to dialogue, each person speaking in role as their new character. At this stage one or two sentences are usually sufficient, as in the following dialogue:

Becky (13) is Spiderwoman; Anna (12) is an exotic butterfly.
Becky: I spin a strong web of silk from which there is no escape.
Anna: Don't trap me. I must finish my dance.

Students are asked to talk about their conversation and to discuss whether this dialogue might evolve into a story. Within 10 minutes of this step, most students are ready to tell/perform their stories.

Becky and Anna decided to create a story using movement, mime, and a pattern of two words each: *spin* and *trap*, *dance* and *escape*. It evolved into a story for the ballet.

Groups of five or six students are given a set of face paints or theatrical make-up. Each group is responsible for making up one person in the group with everyone contributing to the spontaneous or previously planned design. When the mask is completed, the group creates a story stimulated by the appearance of the made-up character. This central figure appears, dominates, or presents a symbol in the story. Stories generated this way are usually dramatic in content and form and are often movement oriented.

Interesting stories result from one student being made up in front of the class. The emerging mask (the growth of the character) stimulates many ideas. The quality of the make-up and the sensitivity of the observations are improved if silence is maintained until the character make-up is complete.

These activities, from make-up to telling the story, take at least 45 minutes.

Afterword

Recently, when I visted a Kindergarten/Grade 1 class in an inner city school, I told the children a story adapted from Junko Morimoto's *Mouse's Marriage* (Picture Puffin Penguin Books) and *The Dancing Kettle and Other Japanese Folktales*, retold by Yoshiko Uchido (Berkley Creative Arts Book Company, Berkley, California).

A HUSBAND FOR CHUKO

Mr. Mouse loves his daughter Chuko so much that only the strongest and most important husband in the world would be suitable for her. He sets out to ask the sun, who tells him the cloud is stronger; the cloud refers him to the wind, who admits he can not blow down the wall. Finally, when he sees a mouse tunneling through the wall, he realizes that a mouse is the husband he has been seeking all along for Chuko!

We worked through the story in movement, making a class wall with our bodies to resist the wind and taking turns at being the mouse tunneling through the wall. We spoke our names to each other proudly, as the most important people in the world. We painted the story, all 16 children squatting on the floor and amicably sharing the mural-size paper. Then they talked about the story painting and the wedding party. We sat in a circle and passed around a small empty basket, each child contributing the name of a favorite ethnic food for the wedding feast.

The class teacher told me she read at least four picture books a day to these children, most of whom were just beginning to speak English as a second language.

In another school district where regular storytelling festivals take place, the children told and retold familiar and new stories to each other and to their guests. Children's stories are printed on colored paper place mats and used by local restaurants to promote literacy!

Young Writers' Weeks seem to be happening everywhere, and storytelling and sharing, readings and talks about writing and publishing are pursued enthusiastically.

MILES (age 6) tells me about his picture: This is my street. It doesn't really have an orange tree. I was just pretending.

TODD (age 8): I have an idea for your next play. When I went to Kindergarten my first time, I was scared because I didn't know anybody.

STEVEN (age 7) wrote to me after a class "Writers in the Classroom" visit: My favorite part was when Geoff and me made up a baseball story and blamed a broken window on our baby brother, but we don't have one of course.

JENNY (age 7): I want to be a playwrighter. It must be fun. *I will make up lots and lots of stories.*

Through their stories the children share their hopes and fears and joys, and bring all of us closer to an understanding of the human condition, surely a cause for celebration.

Bob Barton and David Booth, in their definitive *Stories in the Classroom*, write:

We celebrate the teachers who plunge into story pools with children.

We celebrate the authors and illustrators who write down, retell, invent, and illuminate stories from and for all people.

But most of all, we sing the praises of the story —

that most simple and complex creation of all the arts, resonating from caves and echoing from the moons of distant planets. We are all part of the story tapestries of our tribes, our threads woven into yours, each tale embroidered with the strands of others, for all time.

Selected bibliography

Barton, Bob. *Tell Me Another*. Markham, Ontario: Pembroke Publishers Limited; Portsmouth, New Hampshire: Heinemann Educational Books, 1986.

Bob Barton covers all the essential aspects of storytelling in a clear, concise, and helpful way. Significant for teachers interested in storytelling in the classroom.

Barton, Bob and David Booth. *Stories in the Classroom*. Markham, Ontario: Pembroke Publishers Limited; Portsmouth, New Hampshire: Heinemann Educational Books, 1990.

The definitive book on the subject. This practical guide shows teachers how to find, choose, and use specific stories. Follow-up activities are featured, including story talk, retellings, writing new versions, dramatizing, and thematic art.

Johnstone, Keith. *Impro. Improvisation and the Theatre*. London, Eyre Methuen, 1981.

A 'must' for teachers interested in storytelling, spontaneity, and drama. The chapter on narrative skills is of particular relevance. The book abounds with ideas for freeing the imagination. Written with zany humor by the Director of Calgary's Loose Moose Theatre Company and the originator of Theatre Sports in Canada. Relevant for teachers of 12 plus age groups.

Hearn, Emily and Mark Thurman. *Helping Kids Draw & Write Picture Books*. Markham, Ontario, Pembroke Publishers Limited, 1991.

Contains sound ideas for collaborations in devising plots for stories, and gives student examples. An excellent list of recommended picture books is included.

Neelands, Jonathan. *Making Sense of Drama*. London: Heinemann Educational Books, 1984.

A guide to classroom practice. Contains many good examples of drawing ideas from children. This is a straightforward and accessible account of how to approach drama in the classroom. The book contains useful outline plans and examples of children's responses.

Rosen, Betty. *And None of It Was Nonsense*. Richmond Hill, Ontario: Scholastic Canada; Portsmouth, New Hampshire: Heinemann Educational Books, 1988.

An illuminating account of work with disadvantaged boys aged 8-18 in London. Their retelling of myths and fables and stories is of particular interest to teachers of ESL students and multicultural classes, who will rejoice in the confidence shown by the children.

Swartz, Larry. *Dramathemes*. Markham, Ontario: Pembroke Publishers Limited; Portsmouth, New Hampshire: Heinemann Educational Books, 1988.

Highly recommended for both beginning and more experienced teachers of drama. *Dramathemes* contains 101 practical drama lessons in ten thematic units covering nursery rhymes, story ideas, and scripts. This book is fun, comprehensive, and thorough.

Tarlington, Carole and Patrick Verriour. *Role Drama*. Markham, Ontario: Pembroke Publishers Limited; Portsmouth, New Hampshire: Heinemann Educational Books, 1991.

This is a practical handbook that drama teachers will appreciate for its clear and detailed guidelines and sources for classroom work. Chapter 3, "Creating Your Own Story," is of particular interest for teachers working with new stories. Tarlington and Verriour make 'role' an attainable and valuable method in the drama classroom. A practical book by two master teachers.

Watts, Irene N. *Just a Minute*. Markham, Ontario: Pembroke Publishers Limited; Portsmouth, New Hampshire: Heinemann Educational Books, 1990.

Ten short plays (five to ten minutes each) based on stories from around the world. Includes strategies for oral language, story making, games and warm-ups for rehearsal, brainstorming, imaginary language, and drama as a multicultural celebration. Permission granted to reproduce plays for classroom use.

Index